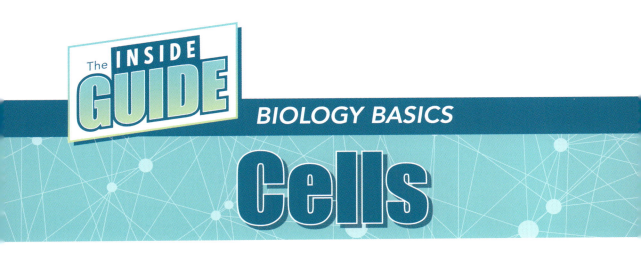

By Leigh McClure

Published in 2025 by Cavendish Square Publishing, LLC
2544 Clinton Street Buffalo, NY 14224

Copyright © 2025 by Cavendish Square Publishing, LLC

First Edition

No part of this publication may be reproduced, stored in a retrieval system, or transmitted in any form or by any means—electronic, mechanical, photocopying, recording, or otherwise—without the prior permission of the copyright owner. Request for permission should be addressed to Permissions, Cavendish Square Publishing, 2544 Clinton Street Buffalo, NY 14224. Tel (877) 980-4450; fax (877) 980-4454.

Website: cavendishsq.com

This publication represents the opinions and views of the author based on their personal experience, knowledge, and research. The information in this book serves as a general guide only. The author and publisher have used their best efforts in preparing this book and disclaim liability rising directly or indirectly from the use and application of this book.

All websites were available and accurate when this book was sent to press.

Cataloging-in-Publication Data

Names: McClure, Leigh.
Title: Cells / Leigh McClure.
Description: Buffalo, NY : Cavendish Square Publishing, 2025. | Series: The inside guide: biology basics | Includes glossary and index.
Identifiers: ISBN 9781502673350 (pbk.) | ISBN 9781502673367 (library bound) | ISBN 9781502673374 (ebook)
Subjects: LCSH: Cells–Juvenile literature.
Classification: LCC QH582.5 M28 2025 | DDC 571.6–dc23

Editor: Caitie McAneney
Copyeditor: Nicole Horning
Designer: Deanna Lepovich

The photographs in this book are used by permission and through the courtesy of: Cover Komsan Loonprom/Shutterstock.com; p. 4 Studio Romantic/Shutterstock.com; p. 7 Yurchyks/Shutterstock.com; p. 8 Satirus/Shutterstock.com; p. 9 Ground Picture/Shutterstock.com; p. 10 Vladra14/Shutterstock.com; p. 12 Dee-sign/Shutterstock.com; p. 13 Ph-HY/Shutterstock.com; p. 14 Kateryna Kon/Shutterstock.com; p. 15 Macrovector/Shutterstock.com; p. 16 VectorMine/Shutterstock.com; p. 18 fusebulb/Shutterstock.com; p. 19 simonovstas/Shutterstock.com; p. 21 luchschenF/Shutterstock.com; p. 22 Quality Stock Arts/Shutterstock.com; p. 25 Prostock-studio/Shutterstock.com; p. 26 Molecular Sensei/Shutterstock.com; pp. 27, 29 (bottom) PeopleImages.com - Yuri A/Shutterstock.com; p. 28 (top) PanuShot/Shutterstock.com; p. 28 (bottom) aycan balta/Shutterstock.com; p. 29 (top) Wisanu Boonrawd/Shutterstock.com.

Some of the images in this book illustrate individuals who are models. The depictions do not imply actual situations or events.

CPSIA compliance information: Batch #CWCSQ25: For further information contact Cavendish Square Publishing LLC at 1-877-980-4450.

Printed in the United States of America

CONTENTS

Chapter One: What Are Cells?	5
Chapter Two: Parts of a Cell	11
Chapter Three: Types of Cells	17
Chapter Four: Plants vs. Animals	23
Think About It!	28
Glossary	30
Find Out More	31
Index	32

How many cells does a human have? Scientists say we have more than 30 trillion cells!

WHAT ARE CELLS?

Chapter One

What do humans, elephants, and seaweed all have in common? They are all living things, and therefore, they are all made up of cells. All plants and animals on Earth have cells, which are the basic units, or building blocks, of life. They divide as a living thing grows, so the bigger something is, the more cells it has. Elephants have many more cells than a house cat, for example.

Most cells are very tiny. However, they perform amazing tasks. For example, brain cells called neurons help send information from the brain throughout the body to help a human or an animal think and move.

Small but Mighty

If you could look at different cells under a microscope, you'd notice that there are differences between them. Some are shaped like flattened balls. Others are shaped like cubes.

Most cells are so small you can't see them without a microscope. For example, 10,000 of your cells could fit

Fast Fact
Some bacteria have only one tiny cell. However, bacteria are still living things.

CELL REPRODUCTION

Cells reproduce all the time. Each cell can split into two new cells through a process called the cell cycle. Cells divide so an organism, or living thing, can grow. New cells also replace dead cells.

In a process called mitosis, a cell is **replicated** to make exact copies of the original. The resulting cells have the same DNA.

Cell reproduction is a normal part of life. Most of the time, cells divide without a problem. However, if cells reproduce uncontrollably and start to spread where they aren't supposed to, that causes cancer. Cancer can cause growths, called tumors, to grow in the body.

on the head of a pin! Even though they are small, they all have special jobs in the body. They keep you alive and growing every day. Human cells give your body structure. They also take in nutrients from the things you eat and drink, then turn the nutrients into energy. Some carry nutrients and oxygen throughout your body.

Fast Fact
The largest cells on Earth are the eggs of birds. An ostrich egg's **yolk** is the largest cell in the world.

A Cell's Code

How does a cell know what to do? How does it know what organism it makes up? The "code" for cells exists in their DNA, which stands for deoxyribonucleic acid. DNA is found in the nucleus of each cell. It carries genetic information, which gives a living thing its features.

All humans have 99.6 percent identical DNA. However, no two people on Earth have the *exact* same DNA—not even identical twins.

DNA is like an instruction manual. It directs the cell to make certain substances called proteins, which determine their growth. Proteins do much of the work in a body. For example, they allow cells in an organism's heart to help that organ function.

Fast Fact
The twisted ladder-like shape of DNA is called a double helix.

Bacteria

Everything in nature has bacteria. These simple, small organisms can only be seen with a microscope. They have only one cell. Bacteria can cause many issues in a body, such as illness and infection. If "bad" bacteria get into the body through the mouth, nose, or a wound, they can replicate over and over until the person is sick.

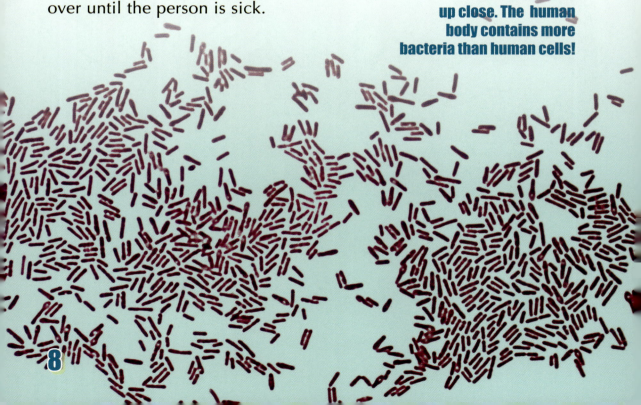

This is bacteria up close. The human body contains more bacteria than human cells!

To keep from getting sick, some people wear masks and wash their hands often to stop bacteria from entering their body.

A body's **immune system** often fights off bad bacteria. However, people sometimes need to take medicines called antibiotics if they get an infection. These medicines get rid of bacteria.

The body also has billions of "good" bacteria, especially in the gut. Gut bacteria help your body break down nutrients.

Models can help you visualize cell organelles, or parts.

PARTS OF A CELL

Chapter Two

Cells are small, and they're made up of even smaller parts. Each one of those parts has a job to do. Animal cells and plant cells have some of the same parts. However, some parts are different.

Most cells have three main parts. The nucleus is like the brain. The cell membrane is like the skin. The cytoplasm is mostly fluid, with structures called organelles floating around. These are the workers of the cell. The parts of a cell work together like a team to keep the cell alive and well.

A Look at the Nucleus

A cell's nucleus is one of its most important parts. That's because it controls the cell's ability to grow and multiply. As the control center of the cell, it directs the rest of the organelles in the cell.

The nucleus is the largest organelle in a cell. Chromosomes in the nucleus contain the DNA that tells a cell what to do and determines what a living thing looks like and how it acts. They are passed down from parent to offspring. The nucleus also has a part called the nucleolus, which makes the

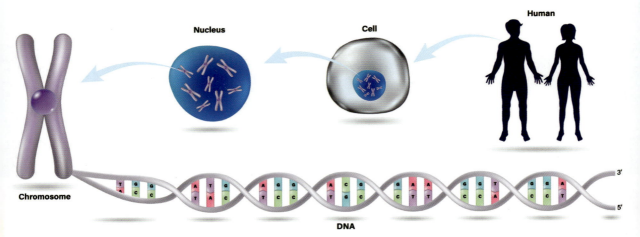

Inside of human cells are nuclei and chromosomes, which contain DNA. Sections of DNA are called genes and are responsible for many of our traits, such as eye color and height.

ribosomes that are needed to make proteins.

Fast Fact
Proteins do most of the work in the cell. They determine the cell's shape, what substances it makes, and how it gets rid of waste.

The Cell Membrane

A cell's membrane has an important job. It lets some things in, such as necessary materials that will help the cell. It keeps other things out, such as unwanted substances that could hurt the cell. It gives the cell structure and lets waste products out of the cell.

Plants have cell walls, which give the plant extra support. They protect

Fast Fact
Special openings in a plant's cell walls allow needed materials to pass through. The openings are called plasmodesmata.

the plant's cells. These walls are usually made of cellulose. Cellulose helps plants stay upright. Next time you look at the stem of a flower, think of how its cell walls allow it to stay upright.

Lipid Bilayer

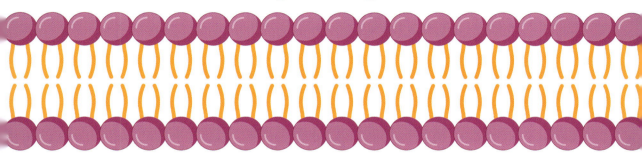

Cell membranes are made up of two lipid layers (called a bilayer) that help take certain things in and keep other things out. Lipids are fat molecules.

Outstanding Organelles

Within the gelatin-like cytoplasm, there are many important organelles. The ribosomes are the factories of the group. They produce the proteins the cell needs to carry out certain functions. Lysosomes are the clean-up crew, removing waste and unwanted substances in the cell. The endoplasmic reticulum (ER) is like the cell's packaging system, packing up proteins

Fast Fact
Cytoplasm is made of different organic molecules, as well as water and salts.

POWERING THE CELL

Mitochondria are important organelles present in both animal and plant cells. They take in raw materials from the outside. Then, the mitochondria make those molecules into energy. They act somewhat like a power plant for a city.

In humans and animals, mitochondria make energy from nutrients in the food we eat. Different animals need different nutrients in their diets. Plants need organelles called chloroplasts to make their food using energy from the sun. Once the food is taken in by the mitochondria, it creates energy to power the cell as it carries out its functions.

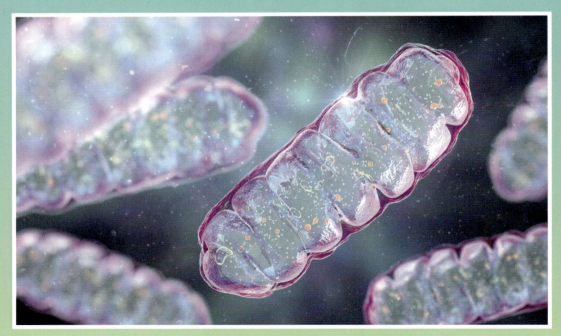

Mitochondria are cell organelles that are long and thin, shaped almost like a bean.

HUMAN CELL ANATOMY

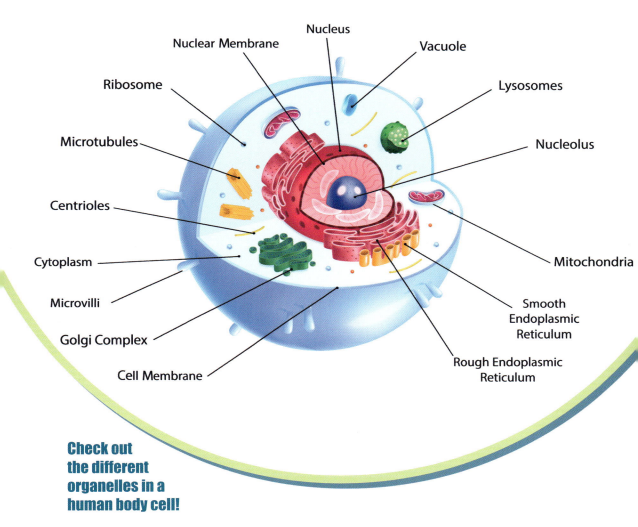

Check out the different organelles in a human body cell!

and fats. A cell has both the smooth endoplasmic reticulum (sER or SER) and the rough endoplasmic reticulum (rER or RER). The Golgi apparatus, or Golgi complex, stores and transports fats and proteins. Vacuoles store nutrients for the cell. Mitochondria power the cell and keep it running.

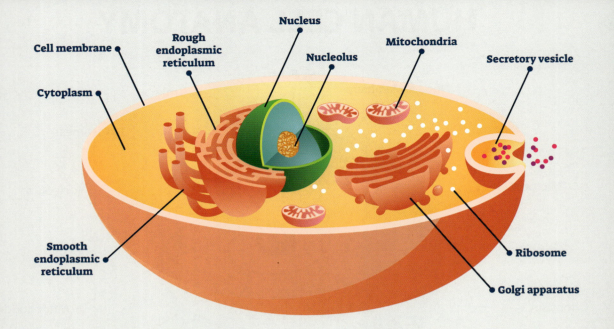

EUKARYOTIC CELL

Eukaryotic cells and prokaryotic cells are the two main types of cells.

PROKARYOTIC CELL

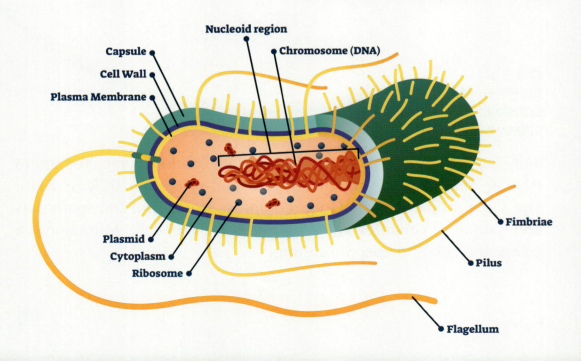

TYPES OF CELLS

Chapter Three

Many variations of cells are found on Earth. Human cells are different from snail cells. Seaweed cells are different from redwood tree cells. However, there are two main kinds of cells—prokaryotic and eukaryotic. They differ in their **complexity** and their makeup. Prokaryotic cells are small and simple. They have no nucleus. Eukaryotic cells are more complex than prokaryotic cells. They are usually much bigger too.

Prokaryotic Cells

Prokaryotic cells are simple because their organisms are very small. Organisms with these cells are called prokaryotes. The most well-known prokaryotes are bacteria. Made of only one cell each, bacteria's cells must do every job on their own. These cells have three main parts. The first is the cell "envelope," which protects the cells with a cell wall, membrane, and **capsule**. The inside of the cell

Fast Fact

Another kind of organism with prokaryotic cells is archaea. These organisms are extremophiles, or organisms that can survive in the most extreme conditions on Earth.

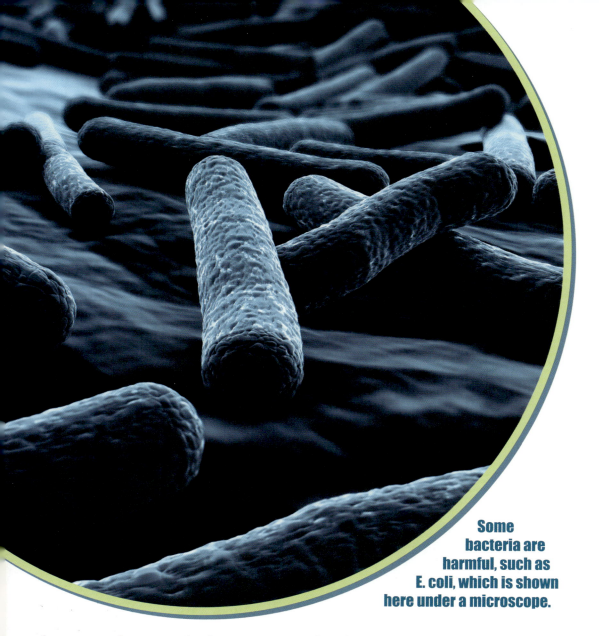

Some bacteria are harmful, such as E. coli, which is shown here under a microscope.

has cytoplasm and ribosomes. It also has a nucleoid, which holds the cell's DNA.

Prokaryotic cells move using flagella, which look like tails. Not all bacterial cells have flagella, though.

Eukaryotic Cells

Eukaryotic cells make up larger organisms, from plants to animals to people. These organisms are called eukaryotes. Their cells are bigger than those of prokaryotes. They're also more complex, or have more parts.

Eukaryotic cells have a large nucleus, which stores DNA. Each cell has a cell membrane and cytoplasm. It also has the organelles detailed in the previous chapter: It's powered by mitochondria,

Eukaryotes include plants, animals, and fungi. A mushroom is an example of a fungus.

KINGDOMS

Scientists put living things on Earth into groups called kingdoms. Bacteria, which are prokaryotic, has their own kingdom. Other kingdoms contain creatures that are eukaryotic. Animals, from the smallest bugs to the biggest whales, have their own kingdom. Plants, from blades of grass to cacti, are another kingdom. Another kingdom is fungi. Fungi seem a bit like plants; however, their cells are different. They don't have cellulose in their cell walls. They also don't make their own food using chloroplasts; they take in nutrients from **decomposing** matter. Some fungi are so small you need a microscope to study them. Others are miles long!

ribosomes make proteins for the cell, and lysosomes clean out the cell.

The cells within a plant or animal all have the same DNA. However, specialized cells have different jobs in different parts of the body based on how the DNA is used. For example, red blood cells carry oxygen throughout the body.

Stem Cells

Some eukaryotic cells are not specialized. They have the ability to develop into many different kinds of cells. They're called stem cells.

Fast Fact

Prokaryotes have been around much longer than eukaryotes. Prokaryotes evolved around 3.5 billion years ago, while eukaryotes evolved around 1.8 billion years ago.

Some are found in small numbers in adult body tissue. Others are found in **embryos**.

Some scientists and doctors believe stem cells can be very useful in medicine. That's because they can change into whatever cell is needed in a body. They may be able to help people with paralysis, or the inability to move body parts. They may also help with diseases of the brain, such as Alzheimer's, which affects memory and other mental functions. However, because stem cells are most easily found in embryos, some people think it's wrong to study or use them.

Fast Fact

Stem cells are like workers who can do any job that's needed. Sometimes they even fix damaged tissue in the body.

Stem cells are immature, or young, cells that haven't chosen a job yet.

Many plants are green because of a pigment called chlorophyll within the chloroplasts, which take in sunlight.

PLANTS VS. ANIMALS

Chapter Four

Plants and animals are in their own kingdoms. It's usually easy to tell if something is a plant or animal by looking at it. However, checking out its cells would give you an answer too. Both animal and plant cells are eukaryotic. However, they are also very different from one another.

When comparing plant and animal cells, there are a few questions to keep in mind. What is the cell's shape? How does the cell make food? What gives the cell its structure? What is the cell's job within the organism?

Plant Cells

Plants are typically made up of the same parts—roots, stems, leaves, and sometimes flowers. Each one of these plant parts is also made up of cells. The cells have special jobs within the plant that keep the organism alive and well.

Plant cells have rigid walls for structural support. They are often rectangle shaped. They have

Fast Fact
Xylem and phloem cells send water and nutrients throughout the plant.

23

organelles such as a nucleus, ribosomes, and mitochondria. They also have chloroplasts, which produce food for the cell. Chloroplasts allow photosynthesis, which is the process of turning sunlight into energy for the plant, to take place. For photosynthesis to happen, a plant needs carbon dioxide and sunlight to create oxygen and glucose—its food.

Plants also need a certain level of hydration, or water quantity, to allow their cells to do their work. Different plants need different amounts of water to survive. For example, strawberry plants need more hydration than cacti.

Animal Cells

Unlike plant cells, animal cells are only held together by a flexible membrane made of two layers of lipids, or fat molecules. They are like gatekeepers that decide what can go inside or outside of the cell. Animal cells aren't regularly shaped because they don't have a cell wall.

Like plant cells, animal cells have mitochondria, vacuoles, and ribosomes. Unlike plant cells, they have lysosomes to digest food and remove waste. They also have centrioles, or centrosomes, to help cells divide.

Animal cells, like plant cells, have a nucleus that holds the organism's DNA. That DNA is like a blueprint for the animal, detailing how it looks, acts, grows, and reproduces.

An animal's genes affect its life cycle and how well adapted it is to its environment. Animals

Fast Fact
In humans, specialized cells make up their skin, inner organs, and brain.

of the same species, or kind, can reproduce and pass on their genes to their offspring.

Sperm cells and egg cells come together to make offspring. They each give some of their genetic information, passing it on to the offspring.

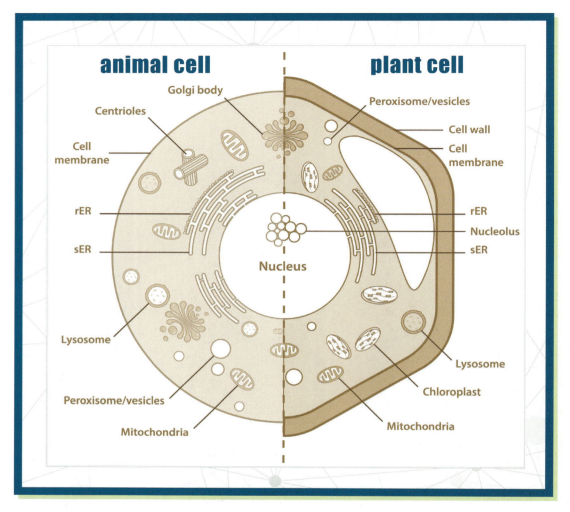

Looking at plant and animal cells, it's easy to compare and contrast them. What's the same? What's different?

Humans are a kind of animal! That means humans are made up of these animal cells. Though different cells in your body may have specialized functions, they all have these same basic parts.

KEEPING CELLS HEALTHY

If a living thing is made of cells, it makes sense that cell health is important. How can you keep cells healthy? Plants need a certain amount of water and sunlight. Animals need oxygen, water, and certain nutrients from food.

To keep your cells healthy, make sure you're eating food that's high in nutrients. Fruits, vegetables, whole grains, and lean proteins are good for your cells. Scientists also believe that moving your body can help slow the aging of cells. You can get moving by playing sports, walking, dancing, and more. This can help keep illness away and give you the energy you need to learn and play!

Fast Fact
You can tell how "old" a cell is by the length of DNA strands and proteins called telomeres.

Water helps cells function and get rid of waste products.

THINK ABOUT IT!

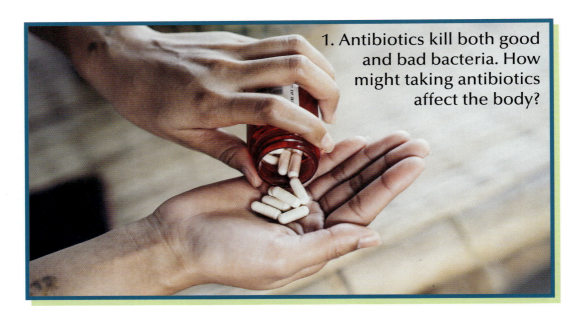

1. Antibiotics kill both good and bad bacteria. How might taking antibiotics affect the body?

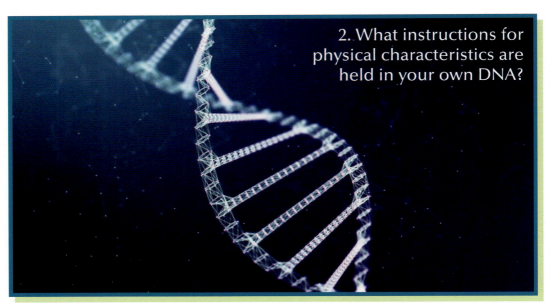

2. What instructions for physical characteristics are held in your own DNA?

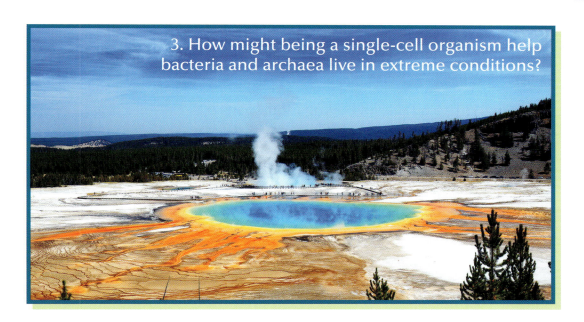

3. How might being a single-cell organism help bacteria and archaea live in extreme conditions?

4. What are some helpful steps you can take to keep your cells healthy?

GLOSSARY

capsule: The outer layer that covers the cells of many different species of bacteria.

complexity: The quality of having many parts.

decompose: To break down through chemical change.

embryo: An animal in the early stages of growth.

evolve: To change slowly over time and across generations.

identical: The state of being the same.

immune system: The system that protects the body from foreign substances, cells, and tissues.

replicate: To produce a copy of something.

yolk: The material in an egg that supplies food to the developing animal inside.

FIND OUT MORE

Books
McKenzie, Precious. *The Micro World of Animal and Plant Cells.* North Mankato, MN: Capstone Press, 2022.

Owen, Ruth. *Cells.* Minneapolis, MN: SilverTip Publishing, 2024.

York, M. J. *Human Body.* Mankato, MN: Child's World, 2021.

Websites

Cell
kids.britannica.com/kids/article/cell/352933
Explore the different kinds of cells with Britannica.

The Cell
www.ducksters.com/science/the_cell.php
Discover more facts about cells with Ducksters.

Your Amazing Brain
kids.nationalgeographic.com/science/article/your-amazing-brain
Learn more about the special cells that make up your amazing brain!

Publisher's note to educators and parents: Our editors have carefully reviewed these websites to ensure that they are suitable for students. Many websites change frequently, however, and we cannot guarantee that a site's future contents will continue to meet our high standards of quality and educational value. Be advised that students should be closely supervised whenever they access the internet.

INDEX

B
bacteria, 5, 8, 9, 17, 18, 20

C
cell cycle, 6
cell health, 27
cell membrane, 11, 12, 17, 18, 24
cellulose, 13, 20
centrosomes, 24
chromosomes, 11
cytoplasm, 11, 13, 18

D
deoxyribonucleic acid (DNA), 6, 8, 11, 19, 20, 24, 27

E
eukaryotic cells, 17, 19, 20, 23

G
genes, 8, 11, 18, 24
Golgi apparatus, 15

I
immune system, 9

K
kingdoms, 20, 23

L
lipids, 13, 24
lysosomes, 13, 20, 24

M
mitochondria, 14, 19, 24
mitosis, 6

N
neurons, 5
nucleoid, 18
nucleolus, 11
nucleus, 6, 11, 17, 19, 24
nutrients, 6, 9, 14, 15, 23, 27

O
organelles, 13, 14, 17, 19, 24
oxygen, 6, 20, 24, 27

P
prokaryotic cells, 17, 18, 20
proteins, 8, 12, 15, 20, 27

R
ribosomes, 12, 18, 20, 24

S
stem cells, 20

T
telomeres, 27

V
vacuoles, 15, 24

W
water, 13, 23, 24, 27